MOTORCYCLE

The Making of a Harley-Davidson

MOTORCYCLE

The Making of a Harley-Davidson

William Jaspersohn

Little, Brown and Company

BOSTON   TORONTO

Also by William Jaspersohn

A DAY IN THE LIFE OF A VETERINARIAN

HOW THE FOREST GREW

THE BALLPARK
One Day Behind the Scenes at a Major League Game

A DAY IN THE LIFE OF A TELEVISION NEWS REPORTER

A DAY IN THE LIFE OF A MARINE BIOLOGIST

MAGAZINE
Behind the Scenes at Sports Illustrated

Second Printing

Library of Congress Cataloging in Publication Data

Jaspersohn, William.
    Motorcycle! : the making of a Harley-Davidson
Sportster.

    Summary: Text and photographs follow a motorcycle
at the Harley Davidson factory from start to finish.
    1. Harley-Davidson motorcycle—Juvenile literature.
[1. Harley-Davidson motorcycle. 2. Motorcycles]
I. Title.
TL448.H3J37 1984   629.2'275   84-14355
ISBN 0-316-45817-1

Illustrations on page 22 by Kim Llewellyn

Photo on page 12 top courtesy of the Harley-Davidson Motor Company

Photo on page 42 top courtesy of the Harley-Davidson Motor Company
  by Incom Photography Company, York, Pennsylvania

All other photos by William Jaspersohn

MV

*Published simultaneously in Canada
by Little, Brown & Company (Canada) Limited*

PRINTED IN THE UNITED STATES OF AMERICA

This book is for my friend
Don Alan Bishop

MOTORCYCLES — THOSE SLEEK, exhilarating, economical two-wheeled vehicles — were invented even before the automobile. Stream-propelled motorcycles were being tested as early as 1868, and in the United States, the first commercially produced vehicles were manufactured in 1901. Before long, a number of motorcycle manufacturers had sprung up around the country. Companies named Thomas, Harley-Davidson, Indian, Yale, Pope, Minnesota, Merkel, Henderson, and Thor all produced vehicles to fit any budget, but only two — Harley-Davidson and Indian — were still building bikes after World War II. And today, Harley-Davidson is the only remaining American manufacturer of motorcycles.

The Harley-Davidson home plant is located in Milwaukee, Wisconsin. The plant employs several hundred people. It is here that orders are processed, bikes are designed, and engines are built. But the real backbone of this process, the element that makes it all worthwhile, is the customer. Without customers, there would be no Harley-Davidson Company at all.

Mike Powers has been riding dirt bikes and trail bikes in Vermont since he was thirteen. He's eighteen now — and dying to have his own street bike. He's saved money all summer while driving trucks for a construction company, and he knows exactly what kind of bike he'd like to buy — the Harley-Davidson Sportster. The Sportster is a lean, low-slung, functional street bike with a powerful 1000 cubic centimeter V-twin engine. It has the lowest center of gravity of any bike on the road, which means better balance and smoother riding.

When Mike goes to the local bike shop to place his order, he decides to test-drive a Sportster before finalizing the deal. The Sportster weighs 600 pounds, but when Mike pulls the weight off the kickstand, it seems to float, perfectly balanced, beneath him. And when he gets it out on the road, Mike discovers that he doesn't merely *like* the Sportster, he loves it. His first sensation upon kicking the engine over is a low rumble jiggling his insides. Then, as he takes the vehicle through its gears, working the clutch grip with his left hand, the shift tabs with his right foot, Mike notes its responsiveness and stability. When you're moving on this bike you don't feel its weight at all! Before long, Mike experiences a feeling dear to motorcyclists everywhere — freedom. With the wind whistling across his face and through his helmet, and a thousand c.c.'s roaring beneath him, and his feet inches above the pale gray blur of road, he feels free.

After returning to the shop, Mike doesn't hesitate. He orders a metallic-blue bike with laced chrome wheels, and gives the salesman a $50 deposit. The bike will be special ordered for delivery in two weeks. Now all he has to do is wait!

But in Milwaukee, Wisconsin, the process of building such a bike has only just begun. Thousands of worker hours go into its design and manufacture. Art, engineering, industry, and technology all play important roles. Back at the home plant in Milwaukee, sales department staffers are processing the motorcycle orders that stream in daily from authorized Harley-Davidson dealers around the country. Computers keep track of which bikes go to what dealer, and somewhere on this computer's floppy disc is the order for Mike's bike.

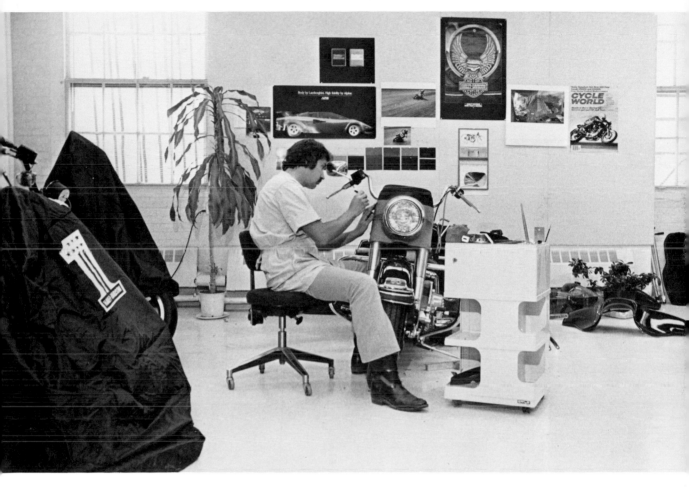

Upstairs, in a sunny suite of rooms on the third floor, industrial designers are working on next year's line of Harley-Davidson bikes, and some of the designs are so secret that drapes are placed over them in case outsiders peek in.

Using modeling clay, the designers make three-dimensional models from precise sketches they have drawn. They may want only to modify the design of a headlamp housing, or change the shape of a gas tank, so sometimes they'll build their models of such parts by layering clay over an existing piece. The designers are all motorcycle enthusiasts. They take into account what customers want in a high-quality bike. Their main job, as one puts it, is to make pleasing and beautiful bike designs that are also structurally sound and functional.

This is where the Engineering Department comes in. The
design chief is in daily communication with Harley's engineers
— showing them designs and asking if they're feasible from an
engineering standpoint. Thus begins the careful, sometimes
difficult process of transforming their visions into shining,
solid, sleek, and powerful machines.

Once a design has been agreed upon (and approved by a committee of company executives), the Engineering Department begins drawing blueprints of the new or modified model. The *draftsmen*, as they're called, are specially trained at what they do. Each blueprint is a precise set of instructions for the rest of the plant to follow as the new bike is built. And the engineers can test the designs in the blueprints by feeding the bike's measurements, or *specifications*, into computers. The computers show where any weak points in the frame structure — or elsewhere — are, and these are then corrected.

If the design is a new one, the Engineering Department can ask the machine shop downstairs to stamp out the bike's pieces on their machines so the Build Shop next door can build a *prototype* of the new model. A prototype is the first version of anything, on which a finished, manufactured version is modeled. Once the prototype of a new motorcycle is built, it can then be studied by Engineering, tests can be run, and further modifications can be made to iron out the "bugs." The average cost of building the prototype of a new motorcycle? $100,000.

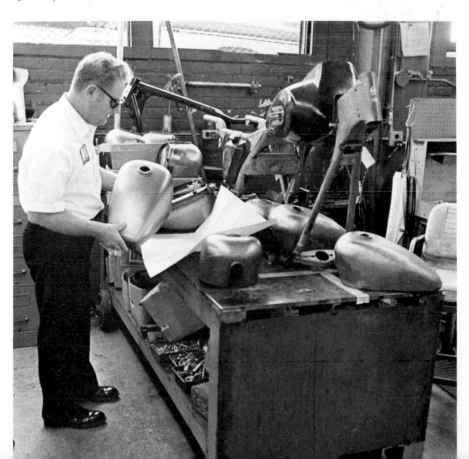

Testing is one of the most critical activities that goes on at the home factory. The company wants to manufacture the best product it can, as efficiently as possible, so it can charge the lowest possible price. The heart of a motorcycle is its engine. With its thousand c.c. and eighty cubic inch V-Twins, Harley-Davidson thinks it manufactures two of the best motorcycle engines in the world. But Harley wants to keep them the best, which means always trying to improve them. So engineers tinker. They make changes. The changes must be tested. And one of the places where old and new engine designs undergo the severest testing is the *Dynamometer Area*, a wide, street-level hall lined with sophisticated testing booths that contain devices called *dynamometers*.

Does a new engine vibrate too much? The dynamometer measures vibrations. Is one series of engine adjustments more fuel-efficient and less polluting than another? The dynamometer tells all. Most important, it can track an engine's performance over a long stretch of time, and under controlled conditions. The dynamometer is an engineer's best friend.

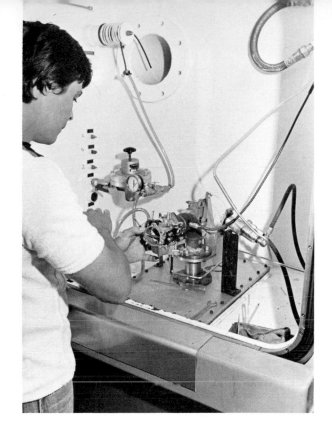
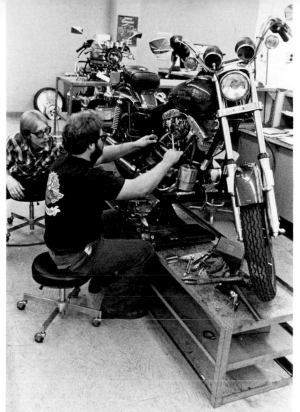

So, too, is the *Carburetor Air-flow Lab*. An engine, in simplest terms, is a power pump. In a motorcycle engine, the source of the power is gasoline. The carburetor serves as a kind of bowl where gasoline and air mix together in preparation for being sucked into the engine's two main chambers, called *cylinders*, where the mixture is burned. The Carburetor Air-flow Lab wants to know exactly how air flows through a carburetor. By modifying the flow rates in special booths, Harley-Davidson technicians can determine, among other things, what amounts of air and gasoline mixed together burn best.

All aspects of a motorcycle's performance are studied in Harley's 365-Day Road Test area. Every day, rain or shine, riders take designated bikes on specially controlled 300-mile rides around Milwaukee. And from these rides, engineers and mechanics chart the bikes' resistance to daily wear and tear.

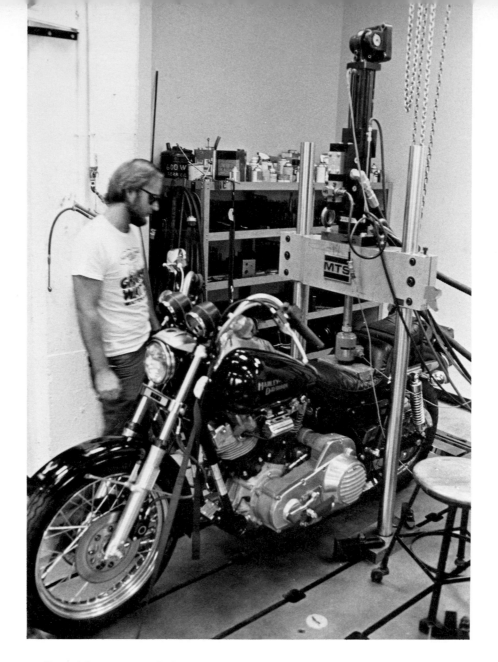

Specific parts of the motorcycle undergo further testing in the *Structures Lab*. To test both seat and suspension durability, for example, technicians in the lab rig a bike to a hydraulic spring device which simulates the up-and-down pounding a bike receives during a ride. By letting the hydraulic spring hammer a bike over a period of days — or even weeks — engineers can see just how long it takes before a vehicle shows wear, and they can correct any problems in new designs before the motorcycles are mass-produced.

The *Environmental Testing Lab* makes sure that each cycle model adheres to state and federal pollution standards. California, for example, has strict laws about how much gasoline can evaporate into the air from the gas tank or any other part of a motorcycle. So to test for evaporation rates, Harley-Davidson's engineers have designed their own sealed chamber equipped with sensors which feed evaporation data into a computer. With the help of such data, government regulations are met.

The "Batmobile," which is actually an Electra Glide fitted with a heavy auto muffler, is one way Harley engineers are studying the engine noise their vehicles make.

All this studying, tinkering, testing, and designing helps the company manufacture the best product it can, so that customer and government alike are satisfied.

The first step in the actual manufacturing of Mike's motorcycle is the engine assembly. Harley-Davidson Sportsters, like the one Mike has ordered, are powered by the thousand c.c. V-Twin engine.

How does it work? Like most gasoline engines, this one is a *four-stroke engine*, with four separate steps in its power-creation. In the *intake stroke* (1), gasoline and air are sucked from the carburetor through a *valve* and into one of two of the engine's chambers called *cylinders*. An instant later, the fuel is squeezed against the top of the cylinder by a fist-like part called a *piston*, and that completes the second, or *compression stroke* (2). Then the spark plug at the top of the cylinder fires, and *blam!* the fuel explodes, driving the piston to the bottom of the cylinder for the third stroke, the power-making, or *combustion stroke* (3). The last, or *exhaust stroke*, occurs when the piston rises again. Lifted by the force of a heavy, spinning flywheel to which it's attached, the piston pushes the burned gases from the cylinder through an exhaust valve (4). The process is repeated, thousands of times a minute, and the power that moves the piston is carried along the flywheel, through a set of gears (called the *transmission*) which regulates the power before it is sent to the bike's rear wheel. And how does the power get to the wheel? A chain (like a bicycle chain, only stronger) runs from a toothed disc called a *sprocket* from the gearbox to a second sprocket on the rear wheel itself. The wheel spins. The bike moves. Mike experiences his freedom.

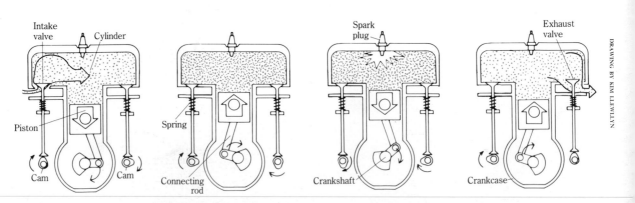

Intake valve · Cylinder · Piston · Cam · Cam · Spring · Connecting rod · Spark plug · Crankshaft · Exhaust valve · Crankcase

DRAWING BY KIM LLEWELLYN

The Harley-Davidson thousand c.c. V-Twin engine and its bigger cousin, the 80 cubic inch V-Twin are manufactured at Harley-Davidson's engine assembly plant on Capitol Drive in Milwaukee.

Engine parts must fit together perfectly, or the engine will leak or malfunction. So almost two-thirds of the plant's eight hundred thousand square feet of floor space is used just for grinding and smoothing each engine's parts to a perfect fit before it is assembled.

Raw stock, such as steel discs and bars, comes to the plant from steel mills throughout the country. But in a matter of minutes, the plant's huge cutting and grinding machines can transform that stock into an engine part, such as a gear shaft, which, spinning in the transmission, will carry power from the engine to its chain-turning sprocket.

Cylinders come to the plant already cast. But before going to the assembly line, each must be ground mirror-smooth, so that a piston can glide up and down within it, friction-free.

Upon being ground to their proper size, many parts — such as gears, sprockets, bolts, rods, and brake discs — are run through a machine which washes them free of burrs and dust in a special solution of cleaning agents and oils.

Pistons go through many different grinding steps to smooth them so they'll fit properly inside the cylinders. Once they have gone through their last grinding and are smooth and round, they are given a bath in hot, caustic soda, which doesn't mar them, but prevents them from corroding before assembly.

Practically every major part in a Harley-Davidson engine is heat-treated. Scientists have found that many metals can be made stronger by subjecting them to periods of intense heat. Since later engine heat might otherwise crack or warp the parts, they are put in baskets before being assembled and are heat-treated in great furnaces to temperatures up to 1725 degrees Fahrenheit.

Subassembly. That is what the process of putting together certain parts in readiness for final assembly is called. One of the most important units "subassembled" before an engine is put together is the *flywheel assembly*. Among its parts are the *connecting rods*, which will eventually each attach to a piston, and the heavy circular flywheel itself.

The rods are first joined together at the base, one rod fitting inside the other like a knife inside the tines of a fork. In fact, at Harley-Davidson, this is known as the *knife-and-fork assembly*.

Then the rods are sandwiched between the two halves of the heavy flywheel. The action of the pistons moving up and down on their connecting rods causes the flywheel to spin, and this spinning power is carried back from the flywheel into the transmission.

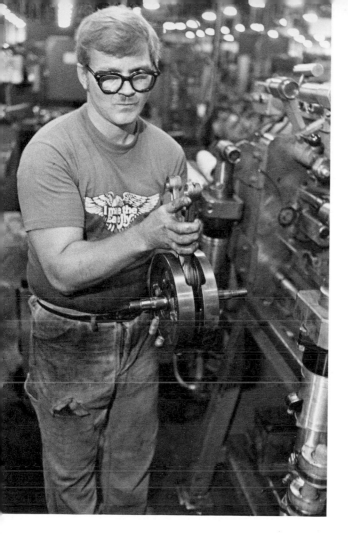

The subassembled flywheel unit is a bulky thing, but it's important to an engine's smooth performance. Without it, the power carried by the pistons would have nowhere to go.

To make sure each flywheel spins without wobbling, it is "trued" — hammered into line by a skilled young man using a device called an alignment gauge and a medium-weight ball peen hammer.

Other subassembly occurs right near the main engine assembly area so that the subassembled parts can be easily brought to the main production line as needed.

One person alone mounts the pre-assembled carburetor to the air-intake passage. It's difficult to believe that this strange-looking unit has any function in an engine, but without it the cylinders wouldn't receive their proper mixture of fuel and air.

Another person attaches clutch handles to long, whippy lengths of clutch cable. Later, the cable will be attached to a device in the transmission called the *clutch*, which enables a rider to shift from gear to gear. Soon, one of these carburetors and one of these clutch cable assemblies will find their way onto Mike's Sportster.

So will four of these toadstool-shaped *valves*: two each go into a part called the *cylinder head* that sits on top of each cylinder. When the engine is running, these valves are the parts that open and close, the intake valves letting the fuel/air mixture into the cylinders, the exhaust valves opening to let the burned gases out.

Four big bolts hold the cylinder and cylinder head together. The finished units are then carefully pressure-tested for cracks and leaks which might otherwise sap an engine's power.

And then the parts that will become engines are moved into place for assembly. No one person builds an entire engine, or for that matter an entire bike, at Harley-Davidson. Instead, many people work along what is known in industry as an *assembly line*, with each person responsible for only one or two steps in the total assembly. In this way, both engines and bikes are built faster and more efficiently, which means the company can charge the lowest price possible for the finished product, while still making a profit.

Earlier, the flywheel assembly, along with the transmission, was mounted inside the boat-shaped bottom shell of the engine called the *case*. Now the case itself is mounted to a J-shaped conveyer bar which moves on a monorail track past each person on the assembly line.

And one of the first parts mounted on the engine is the piston, one for each connecting rod. The pistons are held in place by a stainless steel pin.

To insure a snug fit between the pistons and the cylinder-walls, parts called *rings* are snapped into the grooves of each piston. Without the rings, oil would leak into the combustion chamber inside the cylinder, and the engine wouldn't run at peak power.

Thereafter, every piston gets painted with a light coat of machine oil, which helps make the pistons fit more smoothly into the cylinders, and also serves to prevent rusting.

The engine sprocket, which carries the engine's power by chain to the rear wheel, is mounted next.

Then the cylinders, complete with valves and cylinder heads, are slid down over the pistons. The engine on Mike's bike is a one thousand c.c. type, which means the total volume of its two cylinders is one thousand cubic centimeters. It's called a V-Twin because the big black cylinder housings are twins in size and shape, and when bolted to the engine block, they form a V-pattern.

A few minutes later, another person installs the *pushrods*. These run alongside the two cylinders and, connected to parts in the cylinder heads called *valve lifters*, they open and close the engine's valves.

The carburetor is then screwed snugly between the two cylinders, and in a flash Mike's engine has a fuel-feed system.

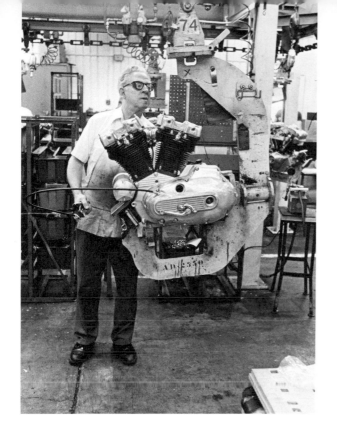 

But Mike's Sportster will need something to start the engine — to kick it over and get it running. This is the job of the *starter motor*. The starter motor turns the heavy flywheel and gets the pistons cranking up and down until the engine starts running on its own. The starter motor is powered by an electric battery, which won't be installed until the final steps of the bike's creation.

For now, the *spark plugs*, which throw the spark to ignite the fuel/air mixture inside the cylinder, are screwed into place in holes already drilled in the cylinder heads.

A few steps later, Mike's engine is inspected. From clutch cable to carburetor, nothing escapes the inspector's scrutiny. If anything minor is wrong with the engine, it is fixed on the spot by a trained troubleshooting repairman. But Mike's engine passes inspection. It is swung off the line. The time it took to be built? Fifty-five minutes on the assembly line, from start to finish. Engines, in fact, roll off the line at the rate of one every ninety seconds. On average, the line produces about 300 engines every day.

Those engines with problems that need longer attention are rolled to an area where several mechanics work called the *hospital*.

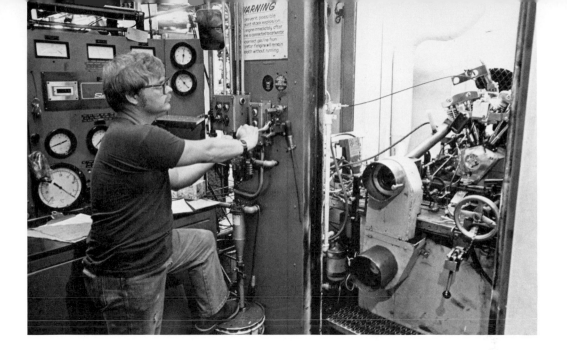

Since Mike's engine passed inspection, it is now started up
and run at different speeds inside a dynamometer booth. If the
gauges on the "dyno" show anything wrong with Mike's
engine, it will be shipped to the hospital for special treatment.
But five minutes later, and only a short while since it was
assembled, Mike's Sportster's engine is pronounced fit and
ready for shipping. In just a few days, a big truck will haul this
and hundreds of other engines eight hundred miles east, to
York, Pennsylvania. It is there that the engine just built will
find its way into the frame of Mike's motorcycle.

The York branch of Harley-Davidson contains 800,000 square feet of work space and employs several hundred workers. Day and night, the plant builds motorcycles that are shipped to a thousand Harley-Davidson dealerships worldwide.

When the engines arrive from Milwaukee, they are stored in a huge, high-ceilinged warehouse full of other motorcycle parts and raw materials.

As engines are needed for assembly, they are taken by fork-lift to a monorail which serves as a kind of conveyor belt to carry the engines into the plant. Somewhere on this monorail today is Mike's engine, the thousand c.c. Sportster V-Twin.

The frames for Mike's and other motorcycles are built in a place called the *Weld Shop*. Lengths of tubular steel, cut and bent to the proper dimensions, are welded together by men using *oxyacetylene torches*. The welders wear safety masks with filtered glass eyeplates as a protection against the torches' blinding glare. Fireproof curtains surround the Weld Shop as an added precaution against fire.

The pipes for the frames, exhausts, and handlebars are bent on powerful hydraulic machines which workers control by a system of electrical switches. There's something awesome about seeing a quarter-inch-thick steel pipe smoothly bent as if it were putty.

But even more awesome are the machines which stamp out the fenders, gas tanks, and many other parts for the bikes Harley-Davidson makes.

They are the "stamping machines," some of them two stories tall. An eighth-inch-thick sheet of cold-rolled steel is oiled and slipped into one press, a button is pushed, and — *karunch!* — down comes the stamp like a giant hand. A moment later, out pops a stamped finished fender.

The same kind of stamping is used to produce gas and oil tanks. Steel sheets cut into ovals are stamped into the traditional peanut-shaped tanks, and bottoms are welded onto each in a special weld department. Then, once the tanks have been buffed and polished on high-speed buffing wheels, they are individually water-tested for leaks.

Frames, fenders, gas and oil tanks must then be painted. How is it done? By means of electrostatic forces! The parts, suspended from a monorail, are automatically cleaned and prepped, then passed through an electrically charged area which charges them with negative ions. The paint is positively charged. The parts pass through booths containing a paint sprayer on a moveable shaft. As the paint sprays, the parts are automatically turned 180 degrees, the shaft moves up and down, and the positively charged paint clings to the negatively charged bike part. In this way, the parts are uniformly painted.

A *primer coat* is applied to every part first. Then the parts are dried for twenty minutes in kilns — huge oven-like devices — heated to 300 degrees Fahrenheit. Afterwards, the finished color coat is applied in the same way, and all painted parts pass through the *Painting Area* a third time for a clear acrylic coat. It is here that the frames and other parts of Mike's bike are painted their dazzling metallic blue.

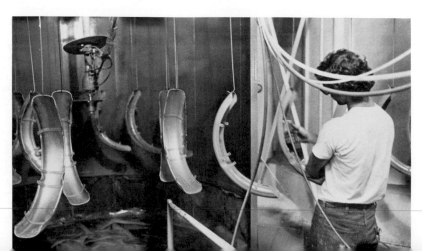

The most painstaking part of the painting process, and still done by hand, is the pinstriping and decaling of the gas tanks and fenders. Special forms are laid over each part, and an oversized pen containing gold, black, or silver paint is run along the form's edges. When the tracings are done and the forms are lifted, decals similar to those used on model airplanes are applied.

The finished tank, with a fuel capacity of 3.2 gallons, looks spiffy. It's ready to find its home on the frame of another new motorcycle.

Meanwhile, most major parts that aren't painted (such as handlebars and exhaust pipes) are *chromed* out back in Harley-Davidson's ultramodern *chroming department*. Before chroming, the parts are buffed and polished to a dull lustre, then mounted on automated chroming racks. The parts on the racks are automatically dipped into a series of tanks, first to be cleaned, then to be nickel- and chrome-plated. The whole process takes about an hour, but the difference between the parts before they go into the tanks and afterwards, when they have been plated with sparkling chrome, is striking.

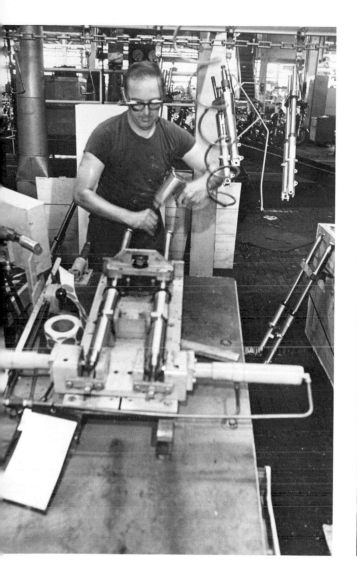

All through the plant, other parts are being readied for final assembly. *Forks* are assembled from an array of prechromed parts. A fork, of course, sits on the front of a motorcycle, and serves as a mount for the handlebars and front wheel. The fork is crucial to the quality of a motorcycle's handling and stability. The handlebars, meanwhile, are mounted with grips and directional signals and wired for the gauges they will receive later on the line. As at the engine plant in Milwaukee, such subassembly helps speed the main assembly process, where speed and efficiency are critical.

Wheels undergo a number of painstaking subassembly processes. All the traditional spoked wheels must be laced by hand, which includes tightening all forty spokes individually. Then, to eliminate "wheel-wobble," the spoked wheels are "trued" on a specially gauged mount, and huge, toothed chain sprockets and solid, flat plates called brake discs are screwed into place.

Next, each wheel gets a brand new tube and tire, and once the tires have been inflated and balanced, they are "flown" with other parts on one of the plant's several monorail systems until they are needed on the assembly line.

The monorail system provides an ingenious way for the company to store parts and keep track of just how much supply, or *inventory*, is available for production. Winding for three miles above the assembly floor and holding over a half-million pounds of finished parts, the computerized monorail dips down to floor-level at strategic points, bringing parts to their stations on the assembly line.

Mike's motorcycle is finally built on a warm, summery morning in late September. Assembly begins inauspiciously enough as the frame is locked into place on a sturdy steel carrier.

Then, a group of color-coded wires called an *electrical harness*, which will carry power from a battery to the electrically operated parts, is clipped into place. And the beautiful, strong *kickstand*, on which Mike's bike will lean when parked, is locked into its slot on the frame.

A few steps later, the big, gleaming, thousand c.c. V-Twin engine, built in Milwaukee and shipped to York, is swung off a side rack and jockeyed over to the line by means of a hydraulic winch. The engine fits perfectly into the frame. Long bolts hold it in place, and some of the wires from the electrical harness are snapped to their proper couplings on the engine.

Every motorcycle needs a footrest for the driver to place his feet on while driving.

For comfort and stability, bikes also need *shock absorbers*, which act like springs to cushion any bumps the wheels encounter.

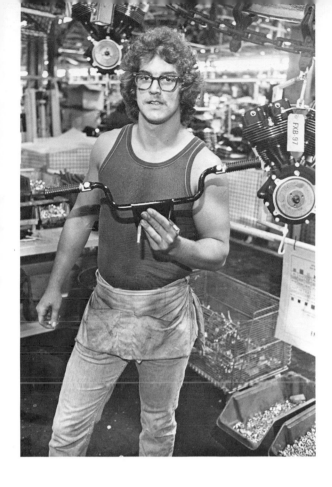

The carrier whirrs, and Mike's bike moves down the line, passing stations at the rate of one every minute and fifty seconds. Along one of these early stations, Mike's Sportster encounters a young man holding a ball peen hammer and a wooden box containing short steel rods called *dies*. Each die has a different digit, zero through nine, engraved in reverse on its tip, and the dies are used for tapping the bike's identification number on the frame and the engine. Every vehicle gets its own number, which is especially helpful to police in tracing the bike if it is stolen.

Next, Mike's bike has its oil tank installed. Motorcycle engines, like those in cars, build up tremendous heat, so oil is pumped in small amounts onto the pistons and other moving parts to prevent heat build-up and keep the parts lubricated while the engine is running. Mike's oil tank holds four quarts of oil, good for thousands of miles of lubrication.

At this station, too, the ignition and choke assembly are hooked to the engine. Mike will be able to start his bike by pulling the choke (which gives the engine more fuel than air), then turning the ignition key (which gets the current flowing), and finally pushing the starter button (which sends the current to the spark plugs). As the engine warms up, Mike will be able to push the choke lever in, allowing the carburetor to receive fuel on its own.

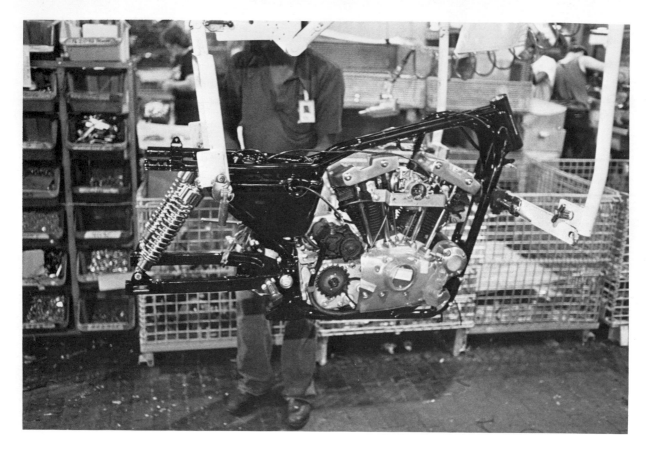

At this point on the line, Mike's bike looks like a side of dressed beef. But as soon as the passenger safety strap is installed and the front fork is bolted into place, the full shape of the machine is revealed. And from a rack dripping with sub-assembled handlebars, one pair of chromed buckhorn beauties is taken by a worker and mounted to the fork of Mike's bike. The actual mounting takes only a few seconds, but afterwards, wires running off the handlebars must be color-matched and connected to wires in the electrical harness, and this takes a little more time.

Two shiny fenders, metallic blue as Mike ordered, are bolted front and rear a moment later. And then the bike "flies" from one side of the assembly line, across a walkway, to the other side. There, the wheels are anchored into place, and the drive chain is connected from the engine sprocket to the one on the rear wheel. Then, a worker installs a small, but extremely important device on each wheel's heavy disc. This odd box with the cable running off it is the brake. When Mike wants to stop his bike, he will squeeze the brake grip on the right handlebar, which in turn will cause small but powerful pincers inside each box to squeeze against both sides of the discs, slowing the bike and finally bringing it to a stop. Disc brakes are standard equipment on most automobiles these days, and the kind Harley-Davidson uses are built to enable the bike to make fast stops.

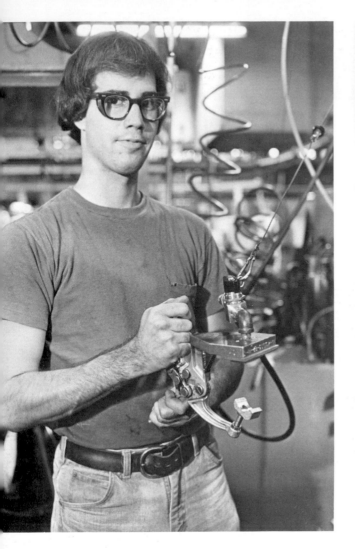

When a brake grip is squeezed on a Harley-Davidson motorcycle, fluid is pushed down the brake line and into the brake itself, causing the pincers to squeeze against the discs. Mike's bike now gets a full dose of brake fluid. It's pumped into the lines by means of an elaborate "gun."

The assembly line keeps moving. Mike's bike receives a pair of beautiful "shorty" exhaust pipes, chromed earlier in the Harley-Davidson chroming tanks. Other parts installed at this time include the headlamp and a heat shield to protect Mike's legs from exhaust burns.

A heavy, compact black battery, installed now, will power the spark plugs, starter motor, and other electrically operated parts on Mike's bike. Another part already installed on the engine which makes electricity when the engine is running, called the *alternator*, recharges the battery.

The bike is nearly built. Other inspections have occurred earlier on the line, but this one is to check the electrical system, the headlamp, and the turn signals now that the battery has been installed.

Then, in a matter of minutes, the gas tank, blue and streamlined, is fitted in its place behind the handlebars and a tube running from the gas tank is connected to the carburetor itself. The gas tank's capacity: 3.2 gallons. Fuel type: unleaded regular. Mileage: approximately sixty miles per gallon.

With a clank, the overhead conveyor draws Mike's bike to the end of the line. Two hours twenty minutes after the frame was first put on the line, the finished machine — all six hundred pounds of it — is rolled into a special booth where it is put through a series of tests. Somehow, what is most amazing, no matter how many bikes enter the booth, is that they run. The engines start. First try. Mike's bike starts. The lights work. The horn beeps. The gears mesh. The wheels spin over the booth's rollers. The whole thing works. Mike's bike actually works!

And then Mike's bike is rolled into a vast area with thousands of other bikes known as the *Quality Audit Area*, and here it takes its place beside nineteen other Harley-Davidson Sportsters. All day, special drivers called quality audit riders select single bikes from each group of twenty and take it for a twenty-minute test ride on the track out behind the plant.

The track is a formidable place, a mile in circumference, with "S" curves, hills, bumps, reverse banks, and a quarter-mile straightaway, all designed to put the bikes through a rigorous, street-like test.

The audit riders, each a crack motorcyclist, are trained in the mechanics of Harley-Davidson motorcycles. They know how a bike should perform. They know how it should sound, how it should feel, how the gears should shift — first gear through fourth — how it should accelerate on a straightaway. They know how it should handle. They are stern critics. No bike ever gets a perfect score. But if a major problem is found in a bike tested, then the other bikes in its group are checked for the problem, too. In this way, Harley-Davidson hopes it maintains the high quality in its machines — a detail for which it is famous.

The day after Mike's bike is assembled it goes through the quality audit ride. It passes with flying colors. "A fine vehicle!" the audit rider writes in his report about the bike.

Mike's motorcycle is rolled, then, to the shipping department, where it is readied for its long ride to Vermont. The seat is put into place but not bolted. Polyethylene plastic is wrapped around the handlebars, exhausts, fenders, and engine. A winch lowers the bike onto a wooden platform. Steel bands are run through the bike's wheels and tightened and clamped to the platform's sides. Ribs are erected. The Sportster is framed, liked an art object, its beauty protected by pine boards. And then a packing carton, big as a meat freezer, is slipped over the framework. Staples are drilled through the cardboard with electric staple guns.

"Call the forklift guy!" someone shouts.

The forklift guy is called for. The forklift comes, and its big paddle-like arms gently lift the crate containing Mike's bike. Trucks are waiting at the depot outside the crating area. One will carry Mike's Sportster to Vermont. Something very complicated and not a little wonderous has occurred. A young man has ordered a motorcycle. The motorcycle has been built.

And so it is, on a cool Saturday morning in September, and exactly two weeks to the day from Mike's first visit, the dealer telephones Mike to tell him that his bike has arrived. Mike says he'll be down before noon, and the dealer and the salesman spend the next two-and-a-half hours readying the Sportster. They uncrate it. They strip off the polyethylene plastic. They adjust the mirrors. They polish the fenders. They lubricate the chain and bolt down the vinyl seat. They fill the gas tank with 3.2 gallons of unleaded regular, and the oil tank with four quarts of S.A.E. 10-40 engine oil. They check all the connections on the engine. They top up the battery with battery fluid. They check the brakes. They do a dozen different things before finally turning the engine over and checking to see how it runs.

"Runs fine," says the dealer.

"Doesn't it?" says the salesman, with a grin.

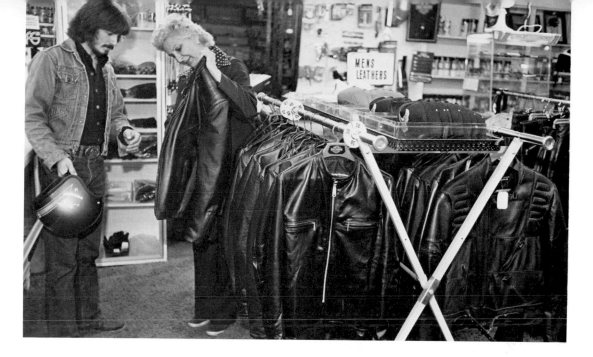

When Mike arrives at the showroom, he chooses a helmet and a soft leather jacket for protection in the event of an accident. Then he hands the dealer a check to pay for both items, as well as the bike, and the dealer gives Mike a temporary *certificate of title*. "We'll send the application for a permanent title to the state," says the dealer. "State'll send the title — your proof of ownership in other words — to you. Meanwhile, don't lose the temporary one."

"I won't."

The salesman has already put a temporary license plate on the bike when Mike steps out to see it. Mike has ten days to get a permanent plate of his own from the state.

"Let me show you a few of the bike's finer points," says
the salesman. And for the next twenty minutes, they discuss
such things as what grade oil to use, how much air the tires
require, how to keep the brake discs clean, where different
parts — such as the throttle adjustment and carburetor — are
located.

"Don't drive it over fifty for the first hundred miles," says
the salesman. "Then take it higher gradually. Of course, we'll
see you for a five-hundred mile checkup anyway. Any ques-
tions or problems, don't hesitate to call."

"Thanks," says Mike. "You've all been great to me."

"Pleasure's all ours," says the salesman. "See you in five
hundred miles."

And so, with that blessing, Mike reaches down and pulls the choke lever and twists the ignition key in its lock. The bike shivers, rumbles, and starts. First try. Mike pushes the choke lever in a hair. The engine idles. Mike revs it using the throttle

grip in his right hand. The engine warms. Mike pushes the choke in all the way. He waves to the salesman, who gives the thumbs-up sign, then Mike drives off.

It's a wonderful feeling owning something you've always wanted. Joy swells in Mike's chest as he downshifts, hands and feet sensing in the bike's rumbling backsurge, the power of what they now control. Road, sky, hills, trees all blur at the edges of his eyes into bands of streaming color. Surging, gliding, spokes spinning like silver coins beneath him, wind and sun in his face, Mike rides, feeling free.

It's amazing, he thinks, that someone or something actually *built* this bike.

Mike rides.

Acknowledgments

I wish to thank all the employees, past and present, at the Harley-Davidson Motor Company who made this book possible. I especially wish to thank Bill Dutcher, Pam Matthews, George Kragel, and Bob Klein (who was my liaison during the photo shoots at York, Pennsylvania, and Milwaukee, Wisconsin, and who became a friend and helpful critic during my writing of the book).

Special thanks, too, go to Harry J. Wilkins, his wife, Barbara, and their son Alan for so generously allowing me to photograph in and around their dealership and service garage and for agreeing to play the "salespeople" in these pages.

And I couldn't have done this book without the help and presence of Kurt Salvas, an excellent motorcyclist, good friend, and splendid "Mike."

Thanks, and blessings to you all.

W.J.